P9-ARS-349

DISCARDED

THE LITTLE BOOK OF
BIG
DECORATING
IDEAS

CountryLiving

THE LITTLE BOOK OF
BIG
DECORATING
IDEAS

287 Clever Tips, Tricks, and Solutions

BY **KATY McCOLL**
AND THE EDITORS OF *COUNTRY LIVING*

HEARST BOOKS
New York

HEARST BOOKS

New York

An Imprint of Sterling Publishing
387 Park Avenue South
New York, NY 10016

Country Living is a registered trademark of Hearst Communications, Inc.

© 2013 by Hearst Communications, Inc.

All rights reserved. No part of this publication may be reproduced, stored in a
retrieval system, or transmitted, in any form or by any means, electronic, mechanical, photocopying,
recording, or otherwise, without prior written permission from the publisher.

Every effort has been made to ensure that all the information in this book is accurate. However,
due to differing conditions, tools, and individual skills, the publisher cannot be responsible for any injuries,
losses, and/or other damages that may result from the use of the information in this book.

ISBN 978-1-61837-038-9

Distributed in Canada by Sterling Publishing
c/o Canadian Manda Group, 165 Dufferin Street
Toronto, Ontario, Canada M6K 3H6
Distributed in the United Kingdom by GMC Distribution Services
Castle Place, 166 High Street, Lewes, East Sussex, England BN7 1XU
Distributed in Australia by Capricorn Link (Australia) Pty. Ltd.
P.O. Box 704, Windsor, NSW 2756, Australia

For information about custom editions, special sales, and premium and corporate purchases,
please contact Sterling Special Sales at 800-805-5489 or specialsales@sterlingpublishing.com.

Manufactured in China

Interior design by Renato Stanisic
Cover design by Jon Chaiet

2 4 6 8 10 9 7 5 3

www.sterlingpublishing.com

Contents

Welcome!
An introduction from Sarah Gray Miller

Welcome!

Some people golf. Others practice yoga. Me? Ever since I bought a Victorian house in upstate New York, my hobby has been fixing up the place. It's a project I hope will never end. The moment I finished renovating a bathroom (find it paired with ideas 129 and 130), I tackled the kitchen (ideas 22 and 23). I've used old mail bags to reupholster dining chairs, arranged feathers in vintage trophy cups, and hung everything from framed book pages to horse bits on the walls. Don't even get me started on the garden: I could spend the rest of my life (and life's savings) trying to achieve perfection outside.

Truth be told, my inspiration comes from the houses we cover in the magazine, all filled with more than just furniture—namely, genius ideas ripe for the picking. *Country Living* has always understood that it's these brilliant, often offbeat strokes of genius that make a place memorable, unique, deeply personal. And what could be more important than that? Our homes set the stage for the most meaningful moments in our lives. They should reflect who we are.

To provide you with one-stop shopping for both general inspiration and specific how-to advice, we gathered the magazine's all-time best decorating, gardening, and entertaining ideas into this handy compendium. We scoured back issues for savvy styling secrets, new uses for old things, and storage solutions pretty enough to double as display. Flip through the following pages any time you're in need of a creative jolt. I practically guarantee that you'll want to scour your local antiques mall for vintage luggage, hand mirrors, and apothecary jars. If you're anywhere near my neck of the woods, you'll probably see me there, treasure-hunting, too.

Sarah Gray Miller
Editor-in-chief
CountryLiving

NEW
USES FOR
OLD
THINGS

H ere at *Country Living*, we like items to show their age. From the scuffed paint of a hand-lettered sign to the crackled finish of heirloom china, patina only adds warmth and a sense of history to our homes. Cultivating effortlessly beautiful interiors, in fact, requires a little chip here and there.

But that doesn't mean we're purists, lighting rooms by oil lamps or using 19th-century tools. Rather, we delight in outsmarting the usual off-the-shelf solutions to create a completely custom look. Why buy an ordinary medicine cabinet from the home-improvement store, for example, when an antique mirror paired with a salvaged shelf does the same job handsomely? Likewise, a midcentury educational chart offers a clever and graphic alternative to the usual pull-down window shade. From unexpected coffee tables to eye-opening lamps, the ideas in this chapter explore the hidden potential of dark, dusty, rusty, anachronistic things, and shows you how to transform them into inspiring—and often very affordable—accessories.

Trust us: Soon you'll be seeing everything from wooden spools, ladders, and hand rakes, to paint-by-number canvases in a brilliant new light.

1. Reinvent iconic Hudson's Bay wool blankets as elegant—and insulating—window treatments.

2. A vintage shaving mirror and a scalloped wall shelf offer a pretty upgrade on the standard medicine cabinet.

3. Look beyond the "kitchen section" to score a handsome island. This 1900s desk became an extra-functional workstation with the addition of wood planks placed atop its stretchers.

Far Niente

19 | 82

Far Niente

19 | 82

4. For a fresh alternative to frames, display snapshots into glass vases.

$5.$ Replacing a hollow-core door with a salvaged (and naturally distressed) looker can change the tenor of an entire space from cheap and flimsy to solid and storied.

6. Used paintbrushes get a new lease on life for this fanciful centerpiece. Simply space two rows of plain rubber bands around a tall, cylindrical vase, then tuck brushes (we used about 40) inside the bands until the tools completely surround the vessel.

7. This sideboard—a $70 flea-market bargain painted pale green—morphed into a washbasin with the addition of a porcelain bowl and a wall-mount faucet.

8. Decant! Decant! Decant! Even the lowliest bath salts go upmarket when transferred to apothecary bottles.

9. Pump up a plain Mason jar. Who knew these classic glass containers could clean up so well? To repurpose one as a soap dispenser, drill a ½" hole in the jar's lid (to fit the width of a soap-dispenser pump which you insert), fill with soap, and start washing.

10. Mason jars also double as drinking glasses...

... an affordable alternative to fancy terrariums...

...and even a bedside lamp! All it takes to turn one into a hanging light is a drill and a pendant-lamp kit from the hardware store.

HAWK

WOODCOCK

CACTUS

DEEP-SEA FISH

ARMADILLO

ERMINE   WINTER COAT

SUMMER COAT

AF
LY

11. Midcentury educational charts replace window shades with something smarter.

NYSSC · A SERIES OF CHARTS FOR BOTANY, ZOOLOGY, GENETICS, HISTOLOGY, HEALTH AND DISEASE, AND GENERAL PRINCIPLES OF BIOLOGY · · · · · ·

FIC SUPPLY CO. Inc., New York, NY

12. Turn a tired side table into a made-to-measure piece by covering the top in vintage yardsticks. For instructions, turn to page 314.

13. Update an antique oil lamp with the help of a rewiring kit.

14. An old chicken crate works wonders as a coffee-table base with rustic appeal.

15. A truly inventive way to display a quilt: Reupholster a worn chair with it.

16. Mounted with L-brackets, skateboards function as playful shelves.

17. Turn hand mirrors into a shimmering mosaic with 5-inch plate hangers.

18. Let an old oar that's lost its twin experience life on land as a salty curtain rod. For instructions, turn to page 314.

19. The key to a pleasing coffee-table tableau? Divide the surface area into zones. Just check out how this $5 flea-market tray magically allows a group of small items to read as a single object.

20. The cheapest accessories are those you already own. Grab a bowl from the kitchen to display photos and postcards. Stack books to form risers that elevate eye-catching objects. Enlist a planter to corral remotes.

21. Consider these three clever ideas for recycling flatware. Use serving pieces as door pulls...

...to tie back curtains with a handy hook...

...or as candleholders. Find instructions for all three projects on page 315.

22. The truth about this tiny, ultra-affordable island? It's just a butcher-block set atop a salvaged machine-shop table.

23. A tablecloth stitched into a cheery skirt camouflages any unsightly items (plumbing, cleaning supplies, and more) under the sink.

24.
Vintage trophies yield winning wine stoppers.
For instructions, turn to page 315.

25. Just $58 worth of hardware—including casters and plumbing pipes—transformed two salvaged doors into a barn-style entry.

26.
26. Elevate dainty teacups into a stunning centerpiece by mounting them on a vintage candelabra. Just unscrew the candleholders; spray-paint the entire fixture white, allowing time to dry after each coat; and attach a teacup to each candelabra arm (plus the center) using a five-minute epoxy. The result serves as a sweet home for sugar cubes, candy, or—what else?—tea bags.

27. A flat file makes a smart, sturdy, and storage-friendly coffee table.

28. Give TV trays a witty makeover. Découpage took this metal folding table from boring to brilliant. For instructions, turn to page 315.

29. Upcycle wine and beer bottles as vases with flat latex paint.

30. Try these three alternative uses for a hand rake. Hang one over a bar and suspend stemware from its tines...

...stash on top of an entryway table or desk for sorting mail...

...or set up a practical tie-and-belt rack hung from the back of a door. You can also adapt this trick to keep your most tangle-prone necklaces in line.

31. Remixed as a pendant lamp, a vintage gramaphone lends harmony to any room. For instructions, turn to page 316.

32. Put your kitchen sink to work as a beverage cooler for parties.

33. Give an old ladder a new life as a place to drape jackets and scarves...

...or prop it against a bathroom wall as a towel rack.

34. A grouping of laboratory funnels adds up to a sculptural centerpiece.

35. How's this for a nifty twist? A spigot-valve handle becomes a doorknob. For instructions, turn to page 316.

36. A nautical rope lends a hand as a witty alternative to the typical banister...

...while an oak log serves as a one-of-a-kind handrail.

37. Recycle your cracked eggshells by using them as adorable—and earth-friendly—starter pots. Simply poke a few drainage holes in the bottom of each shell with a needle, fill with soil, and then sow your seeds. You can even grind the shell shards right into the dirt for a calcium boost.

38. Fashion "fake frames" with two squares of glass bound together with cloth tape.

39. If it ain't broke, don't fix it: This 1950s GE refrigerator still works perfectly— and offers service with vintage style.

40. Go out on a limb with unconventional furniture, like these stump stools, cut from a felled cypress.

41. Perched next to a freestanding tub, a stool provides a convenient spot for bath necessities.

42. Think outside the vase. Vintage wooden spools offer a novel solution for displaying dried leaves or branches.

43. Designed to pack 'em in, a church pew affords ample seating while maintaining the flow through a narrow hallway.

44.

Extend the shelf life of secondhand books by reimaging your tomes as stealthy storage boxes. For instructions, turn to page 316.

45. Discover three pretty-as-a-picture ways to repurpose paint-by-number scenes. Here, a plain pedestal table fitted with one vintage painting becomes a window to another world...

...the drawers of a night stand get a barnyard facelift...

...and a plug-in nightlight sports a bucolic shade.

46. A piece of found driftwood functions as a handle for the door concealing the fridge.

47. Recycle a painted metal tray into an almost-instant message board. Simply attach a saw-tooth picture hanger to the back with Super Glue, hang the tray from a nail, then add magnets.

48. Treat yourself to a sweet serving tray by attaching a pair of handles to a flat wooden picture frame.

49. These trusty wooden clips might be made for the clothesline, but check out how well they hold up indoors, glued to a board.

50. Employed as planters, galvanized buckets and outdoor chairs bring the easy charm of the garden to a covered porch.

51. A little stepstool combines the functionality of a side table with the display opportunities of a curio cabinet.

52. Re-envision three old chairs as one cool new bench. For instructions, turn to page 317.

53. This enamel basin may have outlived its utility in the kitchen, but it stands up beautifully as an outdoor container garden.

54. Two vintage side tables on casters function as a flexible alternative to a hulking coffee table.

55. A vinyl coating (applied by a professional fabric-treatment firm) protects sofa upholstery from stains—and wet swimsuits.

56.

You could go broke trying to fill a big, centerpiece-size vase—or you could adopt our nifty strategy: Set a few small bottles inside the larger container, and suddenly, a handful of stems makes a grand statement.

57. Salvage a damaged rug by having it cut down and rebound into a chichi kitchen mat.

58. Make a birdcage sing a different tune. Remove the cage's base, then outfit it with a basic lamp-cord kit and chain from the hardware store. The finishing touch: a chandelier shade.

59. Candlesticks can do more than just hold candles—they also double as the perfect pedestals for empty ostrich eggs, Christmas ornaments, or other orbs.

60.
Borrowed from a formal dining room, this secondhand sideboard becomes the focal point in a kitchen, thanks to a coat of bright yellow paint.

61. An old mailbox finds new life as a bath caddy.

SIMPLE STORAGE SOLUTIONS

For better or for worse, minimalism does not rule most of our roosts. And quite frankly, why should it? A cabinet of curiosities or a naturalistic tableau packed with varying textures is far more lively than a perfectly clean surface.

Of course, not every essential lends itself to a lovely vignette. The challenge then—particularly in older homes, where storage space is at a premium—is how to create order out of chaos, without having to get rid of all our accumulated stuff.

On the following pages, you'll learn how to disguise a wall-mounted chest with a flea-market painting and how to create a show-stopping, hold-everything tower out of old luggage. We'll help you streamline bookshelves, make your non-working fireplaces work harder, and rethink your closet, vanity, and potting shed in dreamy, decadent ways. And once you determine a place for everything and stash everything in its place, you'll be ready to continue hunting for more treasures to add to your cache.

62. Stacked up, vintage suitcases read as a single unit of furniture, like a cabinet. And this gorgeous grouping doesn't just stand there looking good: Each "drawer" stows off-season stuff, such as holiday ornaments.

63. Create a sense of space with open shelving. Simple white planks and brackets—set against a chalkboard-painted wall—refuse to overpower a small galley kitchen the way upper cabinets would.

64.
For hooks with rustic charm, use a handsaw to slice branches down one side—so they'll lie flat—then screw them right onto the wall.

65. Hide a kitchen cabinet behind a vintage painting. For instructions, turn to page 317.

66. Who says a bathroom can't double as a dressing room? A vintage black lacquer cabinet (for storing sweaters) capitalizes on extra floor space in a practical—yet decadent—way.

67. The ultimate in bathroom luxury: A lounge-worthy sofa, like this corduroy-covered Biedermeier.

68.

Instead of towel bars and hooks, consider using a coat rack as an artful spot for hanging robes, towels, even jewelry.

69. Fill the void of a nonworking fireplace by turning it into free-form book storage.

70. Take
gardening gear from
cluttered to contained,
courtesy of peg rails
and galvanized trash
bins. Then gussy up
the cans with darling
DIY labels.

MULCH

COMPOST

TOPSOIL

71. Try this fix for wayward flowerpot saucers: a vintage dish drainer. The basic sink accessory, which rarely costs more than a couple of bucks at flea markets, organizes a bunch of basins in neat order.

72. Borrow from the library. A secondhand card catalog doubles as a genius filing system for seed packets. Want extra room? Add a recipe box on top.

73. Why waste precious basement space on boxes when you could have a dining room *and* a wine cellar?

74. Put bangles on display in pretty planters. To create the perfect spot for beaded bracelets, cover particle board in gift wrap, and pop it into an antique frame. Then hang accessories from bridal-bouquet pushpins.

75. Driftwood makes an eclectic stand-in for a hat rack.

76. Spice up wooden nesting doll by turning a pair into fetching salt-and-pepper cellars.

77. Solve the dilemma of platters too big for cabinets with a custom rack that displays oversized dishes.

78. A vintage school desk offers twice the surface area of a traditional nightstand.

79. Keep a sprawling collection out of the way, but still in full view, with shelves hung just below the ceiling.

80. White-vellum covers give books a tidy, monochromatic appearance...

...while color provides an organizing principle of its own.

81. Stemware racks put awkward under-cabinet space to work.

82. Solve the problem of unsightly packaging by transferring pantry staples to handsome glass jars.

83. Pegboard and lush wallpaper transform an overlooked closet into a glam home office.

84. Filing cabinets topped by a MDF plank adds up to one smart desk design.

85. Mounted on a wall, blueberry crates seem tailor-made for storing pantry staples.

86. Fruit crates stack up as a wall's worth of rustic shadowbox shelving.

87. A large, shallow bowl offers an ideal stage for ever-changing centerpieces.

88. Plain S-hooks turn a pipe into a pot rack.

89. Exhibit art with offhand élan, courtesy of a clothes-drying rack and binder clips.

90.

Shallow floor-to-ceiling shelves help take advantage of vertical space. For greatest impact, arrange similarly shaped items like fluted vases together, but stagger heights and mix various creamy shades.

91.

Recycle hardware store paint swatches into handy pockets in seconds flat: Stack two same-size cards atop each other, right sides facing out, and stitch together along the bottoms and sides with contrasting thread. Then use flathead tacks to attach your brilliant little organizers to a bulletin board.

92. Humble chicken wire adds subtle pattern and down-home texture to cabinet doors.

93. Attach hooks to a found wood plank for a rough-hewn coat rack.

94. "Embroider" kitchen canisters with DIY decals. For instructions, turn to page 318.

95. A wall arrangement of bottle openers keeps a potentially drawer-clogging collection in full view.

96. A tall plant stand puts bath-time necessities within easy reach.

97.
Arrange beach souvenirs into a stunning vignette by decanting shells and sand into apothecary jars and corked vials.

Caye Caulker, Belize 1995

Block Island, RI 2011

Gold Beach, OR 1996

Isla Mujeres, Mexico 1998

98.

A dress form makes an ideal spot for storing (and displaying) a beloved coat.

99.

For the birds? Hardly. Use cages to showcase plants, books, and more.

100.

This project takes advantage of wooden letters intended for sorority and fraternity paddles. Paint the letters, as well as an equal number of clothespins. Then center a letter near the top of each clothespin, as shown, and affix with wood glue. Let dry before using the clothespins to hang mementos from twine.

101.
Behind these doors? A TV, tucked into a recess above the nonworking fireplace.

102. Show off sturdy woven baskets for holding kindling and firewood. And a few long, lean matches in a vase, for a cold-weather alternative to flowers.

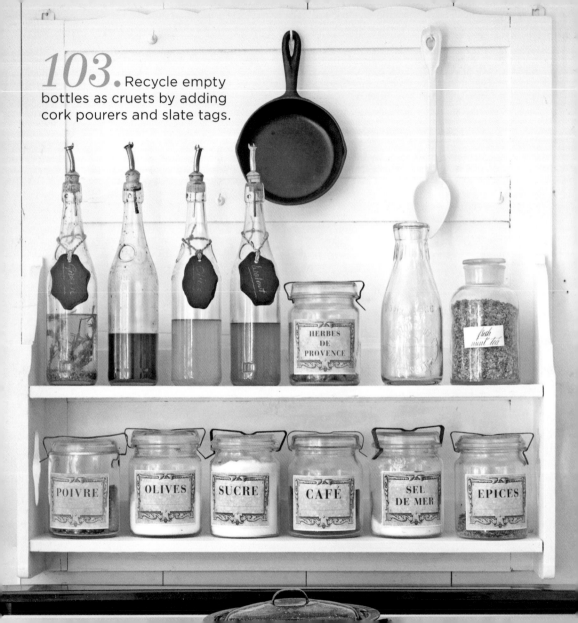

103. Recycle empty bottles as cruets by adding cork pourers and slate tags.

HERBES DE PROVENCE

POIVRE

OLIVES

SUCRE

CAFÉ

SEL DE MER

EPICES

104. A plate rack set in a kitchen island offers stealthy storage.

105.
Repurpose a dresser drawer into a sublime drink station. For instructions, turn to page 318.

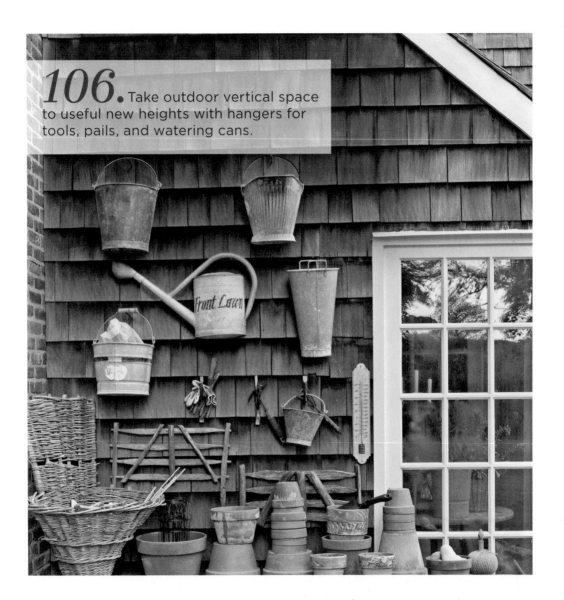

106. Take outdoor vertical space to useful new heights with hangers for tools, pails, and watering cans.

107. Vintage tins offer charming hideaways for pantry essentials.

108. Why buy unwieldy plastic recycling systems when a wooden crate accommodates glass bottles so handsomely?

109. Keep spices within easy reach—and looking good—by decanting them into glass beakers.

110. There's no need to spring for a galvanized metal boot tray when a patterned platter from the kitchen performs the same job with aplomb.

REPLICA OF
THOMAS EDISON
1890 LAMP
110~120 V
MADE IN U.S.A.

MACA

S♥GE

basil

W★SABI

poppy

thyme°

dill

111. Liberated from their cardboard containers, a cache of light bulbs become downright beautiful.

112. This window lineup of kitchen tools makes every inch count, while also trumping the typical café curtain.

113. In this kitchen, the drawer faces conceal a dishwasher and other appliances, while glass jars with clip-art labels hold pantry staples.

114. Painting a china cabinet matte black makes your silver and crystal sparkle like diamonds in a jewelry box.

115.

To create the
illusion of more
space, paint
built-ins the
same color as a
room's walls.

116.

Embrace open storage. Install floor-to-ceiling shelves—accessible by footstool or rolling ladder—and hold tons of tableware.

LITTLE LUXURIES THAT MAKE ALL THE DIFFERENCE

Decorating is in the details: the unexpected twist or trim that grabs and holds your attention and gives any room a thoughtful, considered look. When starting a project, we often begin with the big-ticket concerns: furniture and up- holstery, not to mention walls, windows, and floors. But such major decisions are far from the most delicious ones. The real magic comes through in the tinkering that happens over time: those little tweaks that take a space from merely furnished to fully fleshed-out.

Our homes are filled with overlooked areas waiting for

extra something. Like the humble stair risers that become a splashy focal point thanks to escalating shades of cool, colorful paint. Or the laundry room that's a pleasure to spend time in thanks to a cheery pennant and handsome glass decanters. After discovering how wallpaper jazzes up a dresser or the way a simple stencil elevates a cheap bamboo shade, it's natural to want to do more. So go ahead. Express yourself through the small gestures!

117. Brush a spectrum of shades on the risers of a staircase—one of the first things people see when they walk in the door.

118. Give a chair a new look without reupholstering. This slipcovered seat got a facelift—fast—via a folded, lightweight cotton rug. A blanket would work just as well.

119. A few chalked lines turn a deck into a game board for oversize chess pieces.

120. Age a too-shiny galvanized bucket with a couple spritzes of bleach.

121. Its a given that colorful pillows are the quickest change agents around—but where should they sit? Start with a large, matched pair at the ends of a sofa and then work inward with smaller options in similar shades and motifs.

122. Every room needs an exclamation point; the goal is to track down a conversation piece that doesn't hog the spotlight. This knotted-rope lamp fits the bill: Its sculptural shape draws your eye, even as the neutral hue and natural texture recede.

PEBBLE BEACH

father's

123. Upholstered wing chairs bring living-room luxury to a dining table.

124. Link a bunch of shuttlecocks—in shades like persimmon or pomegranate—together as a sporty garland. Here, we simply lifted the rubber tips and tucked a length of string underneath—to smashing results.

125. Stuffed with
dictionary pages, a basic glass
lamp base looks especially smart.
Other chic fillers: beach glass,
branches, or vintage matchbooks.

126. Get right to the point with photo-realistic magnets, like these fun darts and pushpins. For instructions, turn to page 319.

127.
Ditch unsightly laundry-detergent packing in favor of wide-mouthed glass jars. A string of homemade pennants (fabric triangles adorned with grommets) does its part to shine up a utilitarian workspace.

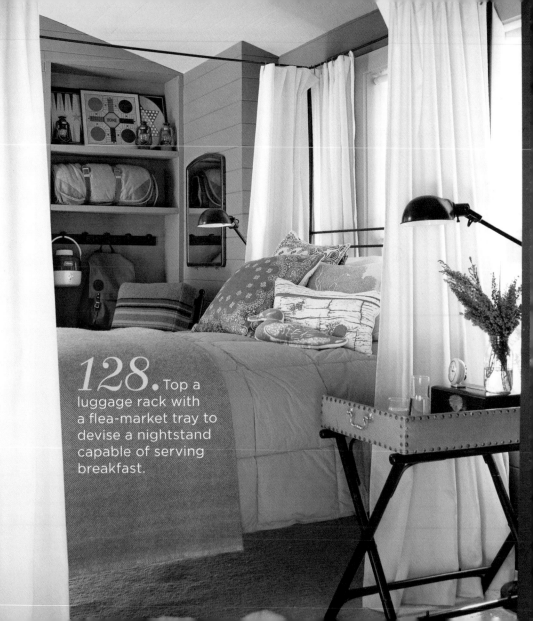

128. Top a luggage rack with a flea-market tray to devise a nightstand capable of serving breakfast.

129. Splurge on the small stuff: Just as a stunning pair of shoes elevates a whole outfit, new chrome supply lines and a European-style hand shower upgraded this inexpensive salvaged tub.

130. Incorporate color—in every sense of the word—with one-of-a-kind finds. Vintage portraits and a funky neon liquor-store sign are real room-changers.

131. Whip up this painted table runner from an everyday drop cloth. For instructions, turn to page 319.

132. Wall-mounted bulkhead lights allow you to forgo bedside lamps in tight quarters.

133.

Turn any chair into functional office seating by adding casters.

134. Pinecones, plucked straight from the yard, take the place of traditional finials.

135. Repurpose cheap plastic straws and colorful duct tape as cheery coasters. For instructions, turn to page 319.

136.
Prop framed artwork on an easel for an unexpected eye-level display.

137. A crate full of glass bottles provides a foolproof way to arrange flowers.

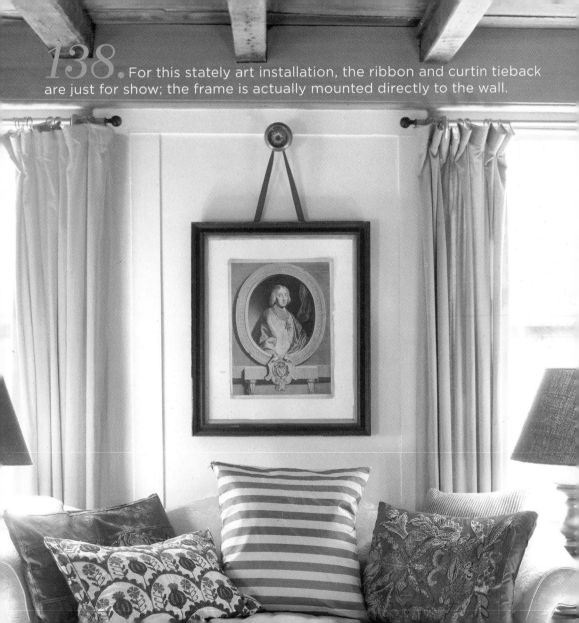

138. For this stately art installation, the ribbon and curtin tieback are just for show; the frame is actually mounted directly to the wall.

139.
Flipping a fabric's "wrong" side face-up, as on these chairs' skirts, can render a bold textile sublimely subtle.

140. Draw attention to the view outside by painting windowpane dividers and sashes a vibrant color instead of the usual white.

141. Try this recipe for a cutting-edge kitchen accessory: Spray-paint a plain knife block white; trace around each of its knives, on the front of the block, with pencil; then paint inside the outlines with a contrasting color.

142. When it's time to reupholster
a chair or sofa, consider uploading a hand-
written letter (like this one from 1882) to
spoonflower.com. Their print-on-demand
textiles make turning memories into
material a breeze!

143.

Make over a plain pendant shade by cloaking it in a wool sweater. For instructions, turn to page 320.

144. Give plain placemats garden-party polish with these hand-stitched floral embellishments. For instructions, turn to page 320.

145. Farm out barnyard toys as candleholders. For instructions, turn to page 320.

146. Transform a dresser with wallpaper instead of paint, for a patterned, professional look.

147. Fall for a new way to do pressed leaves: Capture colorful specimens with a glass paperweight kit (available in most craft stores).

Red Maple
Fox Island, Wash.

American Sycamore
Boiceville, N.Y.

148. Displaying glass bottles in a sunny window highlights their colors—and unifies a disparate collection.

149. Witness the glory of weeds! The beauty of this arrangement comes from a clutch of Queen Anne's lace.

150. Turn a plain-Jane mirror into the fairest of them all—with a frame built from plastic spoons. For an 18-inch round mirror, you'll need a hot-glue gun and about 105 spoons. For instructions, turn to page 321.

151.
Elevate just about any surface—a cutting board, a serving tray, even a door—with boldly hued legs. (Find aluminum and wooden legs at larger hardware stores.)

152. Make a blanket statement and upholster a chair with signature threads, like the Pendleton throws used here.

153. Rather than the usual placemats, try a series of linen table runners placed width-wise.

154. A large mirror makes a lovely substitute for a window above a kitchen sink.

155.Shine a light on the power of découpage by covering the inside of a glass pendant with patterned paper. For instructions, turn to page 321.

6

5

4

3

2

156. Nailed to stair risers, house numbers (here, painted aqua) deliver cleverness you can count on.

1

157. The trick to transforming plain glass votive holders? Humble upholstery webbing. Trim the webbing a tad shorter than the holder's height, coat the raw edges with Mod Podge, and affix with thin lines of hot glue.

158.

Perk up a basic bamboo window shade with a stencil and two coats of acrylic paint.

159. Keep vases stocked with fresh flowers year-round. The key to creating these allium-like blossoms: pom-pom makers in three different sizes (available at most craft stores). Follow the package instructions and secure your buds to thin twigs with hot glue.

160.

Hardware-store staples can easily yield rugged-chic tiebacks. Just combine a swivel-eye snap hook, key ring, and cord.

161. Winsome stamps—like these leaves, skeleton keys, bird tracks, and pinecones—create a whimsical impression on notecards and matchboxes.

162. Boldly-hued candle sleeves dress up a white chandelier.

163.

A buttercup squash can serve as a stunning cachepot for succulents like crassula and echeveria. To replicate this look, just scoop out all the pulp to make room for a pot, then insert.

164. Bypass fussy arrangements in favor of live plants, such as these hydrangeas, that can live on in your garden.

165. Fabric paint and a cute stencil lend a simple pillowcase natural appeal.

166. Turn glass vinegar bottles into vanity-worthy vessals with lovely fill-in-the-blank labels.

hand lotion

facial cleanser

bubble bath

bath salts

167. Hang art on a screened porch by suspending it from the ceiling.

168. Frozen grapes or blueberries give any cocktail the look of a swanky martini.

169. Use a buttercup squash as a candleholder. To create one, trim the squash's stem, then position a pillar candle on top and trace around it with a marker. Then carve out a hole a few inches deep to anchor the candle securely.

170. Dictionary pages—applied with Mod Podge—make this lampshade the very definition of frugal design.

171. If you've got room, skip the bath mat and treat yourself to a real rug.

172. Stacked under a glass cloche, even simple skeins of yarn resemble sculpture.

173. No flowers necessary: A couple of large fronds are all it takes to make a dramatic statement.

VICTORIA
TRAFALGAR SQUARE
REGENT STREET
PARLIAMENT SQUARE
NOT IN SERVICE
SPECIAL RAILWAY SERVICE

174. Colorful sleeves eliminate the need for coasters—and silly wine charms. Measure the diameter of a glass's base, then cut two slightly larger felt circles. Cut an X across the middle of one circle before stitching it atop the other.

175. Looking for an attractive way to wrap up leftovers? Disguise cheap storage containers with custom-stamped fabric covers. Measure the lids of plastic bowls. Next, use pinking shears to cut cloth circles that measure several inches wider than the lids they'll cover. Press alphabet stamps in fabric ink to paint playful phrases in the center of each circle.

More, please!

176. Share the secrets to Aunt Karen's pecan pie by downloading our index-card template (at country living.com/index card). Paste it into a Word document, and type your recipe in a text box atop the image. Then print out a bunch for guests to take home.

AUNT KAREN'S PECAN PIE

3 eggs, well beaten
¾ C light brown sugar
¾ C dark Karo syrup
¼ t salt
1 t vanilla

3 T melted butter
2/3 C pecan halves

Single pie crust for a 9" pie

Preheat oven to 400 degrees. To well-beaten eggs, add the rest of the ingredients. Pour into unbaked pie shell. Bake for 10 minutes. Reduce oven to 325 and bake for 35 minutes longer. Cool on wire rack.

177. This Union Jack gets its British accent courtesy of a Union Jack, applied with spray paint atop an outdoor rug.

178. For a party, wrap small bouquets in Kraft paper and group them in galvanized buckets, where they'll double as décor and favors for guests.

Help yourself to a bunch!

179. Create
refreshing drink
umbrellas out of
paper doilies. For
instructions, turn
to page 321.

180. Stitch up picture-perfect throw pillows, thanks to old family photos and cool printer-friendly fabric. For instructions, turn to page 321.

181.
These ship-shape napkin holders originally started out as curtain rings! For instructions, turn to page 322.

182. Planted with native ferns, the roof of this duck house isn't just attractive; it's a raised garden bed.

183.
Expose a hint of elegant fabric on an area that won't see spills—the *back* of a dining chair. While you're at it, go ahead and use sponge-friendly pleather for the front.

184. An elegant tassel brings refinement to a rugged wooden toolbox.

The Great Naturalists

R O O M S R

185. Wring serious style from an oft-overlooked area! What many folks would write off as a skinny shelf support (left) delivers an opportunity to spotlight tintype photographs.

HOME SIMPLE

SCANDINAVIA LIVING DESIGN

THE ROMANCE OF BRITISH COLONIAL STYLE

New York Living LISA LOVATT-SMITH WEIDENFELD & NICOLSON

RURAL ESCAPES

GAYNOR HAAVISTO GOLDSTEIN RUSSIAN HOUSES

Living in NORWAY

Jean Marie Rome de Montclos HISTOIRE DE L'ARCHITECTURE FRANÇAISE De la Renaissance à la Révolution

American Farmhou

Katsura imperial villa a. isozaki m. matsumura m. speidel b. taut w. gropius k. tange f. dal co edited by v. ponciroli

Old Houses

LALANDE & TOLLAND The New Eighteenth-C

STAFFORD CLIFF GILLES DE CHABANEIX THE WAY WE

HANDCRAFTED MODERN

186. Blinds alone will provide privacy, but the addition of drapes creates contrast and a sense of depth for a polished feel.

187. Arrange a natural tableau with beach souvenirs, whether scavenged or purchased at a craft store. Start with the tallest object in the center, then fan out from there.

188. Fake a fireplace: Attaching a mantel to the wall is an easy, inexpensive way to add architectural interest.

189. For favors sure to spark conversation, craft these mini-candles: Fill acorn caps with melted wax, insert short wicks, and let cool for an hour before placing in a wood box. Glue a bit of sandpaper to the box to function as a match striker.

190. A feather lends a place card fine finish. Simply hot-glue a bar pin to the back of a feather, then hot-glue a magnet to a cork. Finally, slide a place card between the feather and the cork magnet. Bonus: Guests can wear the feather as a brooch later!

191. Call in an overhead picture light to give an inexpensive map the glamorous gallery treatment.

192. Instead of rewiring an old lamp, like this antler version, outfit the sockets with candle cups for a witty, easy fix.

193. The basic components of this cheerful pendant: a paper globe and approximately 75 cocktail umbrellas. For instructions, turn to page 322.

194. A newel post presents a great display opportunity for a lantern, a trophy, even a pheasant.

195. "Monogram" your own napkins with stamps and fabric paint.

196.

Streamline a buffet set-up by popping utensils in terra-cotta pots.

197.

And, for a simple labeling system, use chalk—it wipes right off.

198. How's this for an awesome alternative to the formal four-poster? Platform beds suspended from the ceiling recall front-porch swings.

199. A blah window box gets a fresh outlook, via birch bark attached with waterproof epoxy.

200. Why stop at one porch light when a pair adds sublime symmetry?

201. Uncomplicate your buffet prep by sticking Post-it notes on empty platters and bowls, indicating which finished dish goes where.

HAM

SHRIMP SKEWERS

BISCUITS

202. A few casually displaced paintings lend any kitchen effortless refinement.

203. Don't overlook the ceiling! Wallpaper with a cloud-and-bird theme evokes an open sky.

204. So brilliant, so quick: Inject architectural interest by propping an ornate oval frame atop a modest rectangular mirror.

205. A built-in ledge doubles as an unobtrusive workstation.

206. To save big on the right lamp, hit the "wrong" department. This outdoor fixture cost just $40 at Lowe's!

207. Attitudinal accessories, like a Masonic hat and golf-tee necklace, lend levity to a formal bust.

208.
A little quirk never hurts. This vintage print of bow-tie connoisseur Abe Lincoln steals the show.

209. The secret to an evocative, no-fail vignette: assembling disparate objects that share the same hue.

210.
This wing chair and sofa were upholstered in hardware-store drop cloths, which mimic the look of linen for much, much less.

211.
A hanging socket plus a bamboo garden lantern equals a pendant lamp with organic appeal.

212. The genius of this linoleum floor? It's a brilliant blue.

213. A linen tablecloth draped over an upholstered headboard adds a subtle sense of depth.

214. Triple the practicality of a kids' room by furnishing it with three twin beds.

215.

Here's a cost-cutting idea for hanging curtains: try eyehooks and a length of wire from the hardware store, or a curtain-wire kit from IKEA.

216.
Give an otherwise neutral room an unexpected burst of color and pattern with an eye-catching rug.

217.
Extra-tall headboards covered in a graphic ikat print became an instant focal point for a bedroom.

218. If you replace a coffee table with a pedestal version, you get a living room that functions like a dining room.

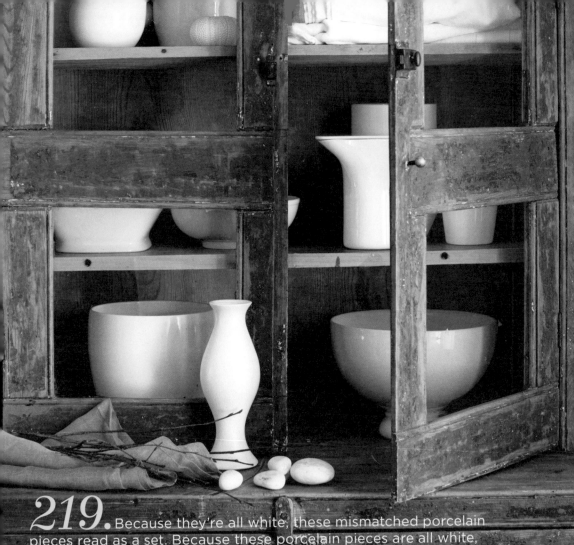

219. Because they're all white, these mismatched porcelain pieces read as a set. Because these porcelain pieces are all white, they read as a set—one that really pops against this cabinet's distressed blue-green finish.

220. Dining chairs become dramatic when each is painted a slightly different shade.

221. A pair of curtains and a small ladder recast an awkward hallway loft as a cozy nook for napping.

222. A painted floor is pretty. A painted floor with stripes? Now, that's sensational.

223. Loosen up a traditional bedroom with mismatched quilts.

GLORIOUS GARDEN INSPIRATION

Making a house into a home isn't just about interior decorating. What's outside deserves attention, too. More than a mere collection of plants, a garden offers fertile ground for creativity and personal expression. Think in terms of outdoor rooms, with walls and floors and furniture, and you'll understand how a lattice-covered fence, heavy with wisteria, can provide aesthetic joy to rival any wallpaper... how two bold chairs harness the power of a river view... how a hedge of grasses, not prim boxwood, softly delineates one area from another.

Ultimately, a landscape is a series of choices, and the ones made by the gardeners featured in this chapter are stylish and smart. A parterre, planted with nothing more than boxwood and lavender, blends formality with fuss-free ease. And the common, and oft-derided, groundcover pachysandra becomes a sophisticated carpet. Let it be said, some of these ideas take time—lots of it— and plenty of effort. But the payoff delivers big, year in and year out.

224.
A continuous line of birdhouses provides the suggestion of a garden wall.

225.

Don't overlook the wow potential of pedestrian plants. This pachysandra, 'Green Sheen', boasts leaves that look like they're coated with lacquer for a no-maintenance ground cover that shines year-round.

226. Think outside the boxwood. Instead of the usual prim suspects (privet and holly) consider composing hedges with tall, breezy grasses for a fluid, almost musical effect.

227. Not only does a stand of inexpensive ornamental grass look good year-round, it also affords privacy without blocking views.

228. Limiting the palette of a border to mostly chartreuse yellow and greens—and choosing plants for foliage and form, rather than fleeting flowers—highlights contrasting shapes and textures.

229. Avoid the temptation to snap up every variety that catches your eye. This lavish look required just two types of climbing rose: "William Baffin" and "New Dawn."

230. Why bother perfecting a complicated mixed border when a profusion of Shasta daisies can be so darn gorgeous.

231. Double your investment with a fence that also serves as a trellis.

232. A workaday storage shed morphs into a garden getaway with the addition of French doors and sheets of wattle fencing that form a faux thatched roof, punctuated by a pair of urns.

233. For refined raised beds, face utilitarian wooden frames with ornamental willow fencing—the outdoor equivalent of icing a cake. Just be sure to stain the boxes before nailing on the fencing so the interior lumber won't peek through.

234. Formal doesn't have to mean difficult. Composed solely of boxwood and lavender, this parterre is twice as elegant and one-tenth as much work as normal beds.

235. Bypass furniture that blends into the landscape if you hope to draw attention to a view. These vibrant chairs practically point to the river beyond.

WALL
ART FOR A
SONG

One of the biggest conundrums of any room is how to fill that empty expanse over the sofa, to say nothing of the areas above beds and chair rails, along hallways, or up a staircase. Our homes are made up of walls—vast swaths of them—and left empty, those spaces can feel unfinished. The most common solution, large-scale artwork, also tends to be the most expensive. Since 10 big paintings will quickly wipe out anyone's decorating budget, the challenge, then, becomes spotting alternatives with the potential to pack a visual punch.

But how do you recognize such diamonds-in-the-rough? The best way to learn that skill is by example. And this chapter is chock full of 'em, with all kinds of bargains serving as bona-fide objects d'art. Tennis rackets make a sporty statement in one room; in another, paper butterflies pose as pricey, mounted specimens. Elsewhere, feathers, book pages, even skeins of yarn climb the walls. These inspired touches establish a far more personal stamp— precisely because they think outside the standard frame. Draw on the inspiration that follows to curate your own gallery.

236.
Even a small display of insects can fetch $100 in an antiques store. But you can fake the look with die-cut paper butterflies that cost pennies a piece (ours came from D. Blumchen & Company). Simply pop the imposters inside Riker mounts, secure with glue, and hang.

237.
The secret to this subtle yet super-stylish wall treatment? Ceiling medallions installed using adhesive caulk.

238. Create

a glorious rotating display by liberating skeins of yarn and fabric scraps from a drawer. The former hang on hardware store hooks; the latter enliven a steel magazine rack.

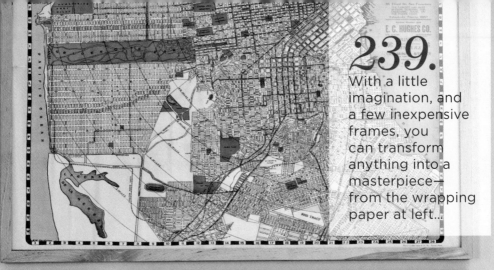

239.

With a little imagination, and a few inexpensive frames, you can transform anything into a masterpiece—from the wrapping paper at left...

...to this bovine placemat...

...to these letterpress greeting cards (above left).

240.

Even a paper bag (this one's from a Paris bakery) becomes art when framed.

241. A single book, *Art Forms in Nature,* supplied all the artwork for this stairwell.

242. A
wall of gathered
wildflowers, dried
and highlighted
against dark
backgrounds,
provide a
dramatic touch...

...as do
architectural
blueprints.

243. In a child's room, a set of vintage alphabet cards adds up to a big artistic statement.

244. Maps creatively chronicle one family's travels.

245. Flank a portrait with hand mirrors to scale up the impact of both.

246. Let curtains run the length of the wall.

247. Repaint old shutters in various shades to add drama to this dining room.

248.
Design your own wallpaper pattern—using photos, postcards, or snapshots of funky collectibles—at tempaperdesigns.com. Bonus: The wallpaper's removable, peeling off easily when you want a new look.

249. The frayed edges of this 1909 map bring aged interest to a white room.

250.

Two discarded windows, casually propped on a table, take the place of paintings in a foyer.

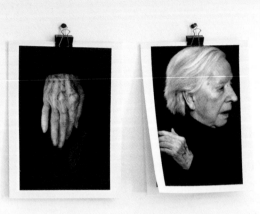

251. Exhibiting photos with push pins and binder clips yields offhand glamour.

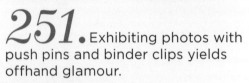

252. Vintage Ukranian newspapers imbue a bathroom with graphic appeal. The pages were adhered using wallpaper paste and sealed with Liquitex matte medium.

253. Flora and fauna thrive in a tight space—as evidenced by these science book pages...

...or ones from *The Book of Botanical Prints: The Complete Plates*...

...or from a book of bird prints.

254. Chalkboard paint gives these black stripes an ultra-matte finish.

255. This woodland pattern is the work of paint, inked out with double-roller from rollerwall.com. As you drag the tool down a wall, a patterned rubber roller picks up a thin, uniform layer of paint from a foam roller.

256. A stencil created this old-fashioned damask pattern; red paint makes it modern.

257. The upholstered wall goes kid-friendly with easy-to-clean oilcloth, stapled in place.

258.
A gallery-esque wall of picture ledges provides the freedom to swap items in and out with ease.

259. Show off antique garments and artwork on a Shaker-style peg rack with a shelf up top.

260. Whitewashed frames unite, and elevate, a collection of paint-by-numbers art.

261. Durable enamelware plates bring interior panache out to the porch.

262.

Well-loved tennis rackets net bigtime style points.

263.
Group multiples for maximum impact. Pompeii postcards wow, when affixed to canvas with bookbinders glue.

264. Tucked inside a shadow box, a cache of prize ribbons looks luxe.

265.

Chalkboard paint creates a changeable canvas in this bathroom. The doorknob is real; the "wainscoting" and "wallpaper" were drawn with chalk.

266. Upside-down parasols pick up on the vibrant hues of a vintage poster.

267. Dress up any regular mirror with a handy stencil and some paint. For instructions, turn to page 322.

268.

Clothespins clipped to a length of fishing wire show off unframed works with easygoing charm.

269. Display art against a tiled wall by suspending it, via wire, from sheetrock above.

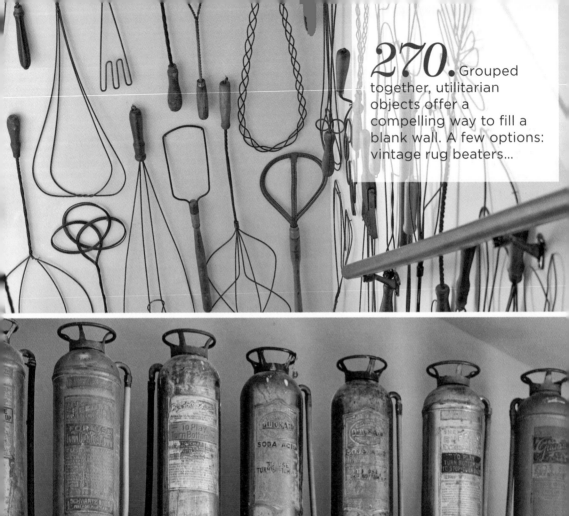

270.
Grouped together, utilitarian objects offer a compelling way to fill a blank wall. A few options: vintage rug beaters...

...old fire extinguishers...

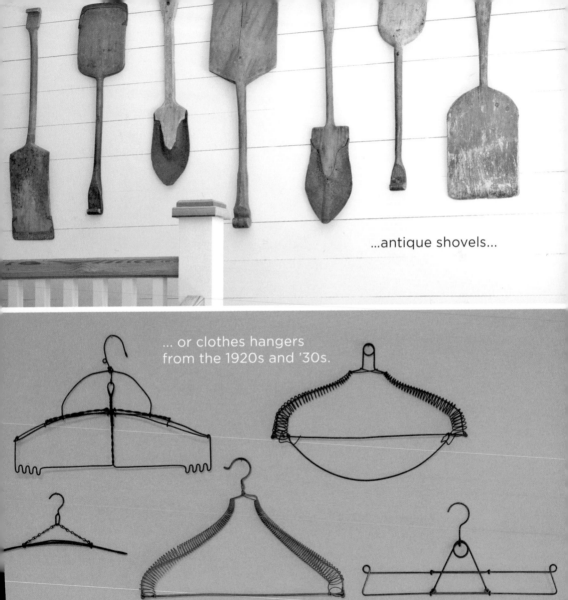

...antique shovels...

... or clothes hangers from the 1920s and '30s.

271.

Even an assortment of grab-and-go sun hats is capable of turning heads.

272. Chanel No. 5 magazine ads offer a cheeky way to fancy up a bathroom.

273.

Vividly-hued folk art and carnival finds, like this vintage number wheel, bring the "funhouse" to your house.

274.
Roosting indoors, a collection of birdhouses delivers graphic punch to the little-used space above doorways.

275. Palm-print wallpaper, especially when paired with a capiz-shell pendant lamp, imbues even a land-locked bedroom with a vacation-villa vibe.

276. Transform inexpensive Kraft paper into moody—and durable—wallpaper, with a coat of varnish.

277.

A dramatic palette, like this two-tone paint job, turns a transitional space into a memorable one.

278.

Add even more personality with a slew of family photos.

279. Designating an entire wall as a floor-to-ceiling chalkboard injects an extra dose of fun to a kid's room.

280. Horizontal beadboard makes a narrow room appear wider.

281.
Catapult a stone fireplace surround to a stylish new place with a layer of white paint.

282. A window frame from an old barn runs circles around ordinary wall art.

283. Fun meets functional in the form of a fanciful little shelf.

284. High-gloss paint brightens tight spaces—such as this enclosed bed.

285.

Dress up plain furniture by surrounding it with striking, artistic wallpaper.

286. A saturated, look-at-me shade turns an awkwardly-shaped wall into an asset.

287.

Moody black paint throws pale pieces into sharp relief.

How-to Instructions

Everything you need to make the projects shown in this book.

Idea 12 Yardstick Table: For a 19-by-17-inch table like the one shown, you'll need about 16 yardsticks of the same thickness. **STEP 1** To figure out how best to align the sticks, create a template of the tabletop by tracing it onto a sheet of paper. Arrange the rulers on the template, marking where you'll need to cut so they fit the width and length of the table. **STEP 2** Make the cuts with a hacksaw or small electric saw. Smooth out any rough edges with medium-grit sandpaper. **STEP 3** Attach one of the ruler segments to the top of the table lengthwise by hammering a flat-head nail in at each end. Repeat in rows until the entire surface is covered. **STEP 4** Apply several layers of clear shellac, allowing ample time for drying between coats. Once you're done, let the table dry for another 48 hours before sitting anything on its surface.

Idea 18 Oar Curtain Rod: STEP 1 Hold the narrow part of an oar across your window to make sure it's long enough. **STEP 2** You'll need two semicircular curtain-rod brackets that are open at the top. Position the brackets above the outer corners of the window frame, and then screw them to the wall. **STEP 3** Attach your curtain, using rings with alligator clips: Thread the rings onto the oar, snap the alligator clips onto the curtain at evenly spaced intervals, and hoist the oar onto the brackets.

Idea 21 Fork-and-Spoon Door Pull: You'll need two same-size serving pieces. **STEP 1** Flip one facedown, then apply bonding glue to the flat end of a one-inch aluminum screw post (available at screwpost.com). Quickly press the post to the base of the flatware's handle (approximately a half inch from the end), and hold until a bond forms. Let dry for 20 minutes. **STEP 2** At the serving end of the utensil, find the flattest point to glue on a second post (approximately two inches in from the end). Let dry, then repeat for second utensil. **STEP 3** Remove your existing cabinet hardware and drill new holes, if necessary, to correspond with the posts. Finish by screwing flatware into place from the inside of the doors.

Idea 21 Curtain Tie-Back: You'll need two same-size serving pieces. **STEP 1** Drill a small hole approximately one inch in from the end of the fork's handle. **STEP 2** Hold the utensil face up, then use pliers to bend the prongs back toward the handle, making sure to form a rounded C shape rather than a V. Finish by screwing the tieback into your window molding.

Idea 21 Utensil Candleholders: You'll need two same-size serving pieces. **STEP 1** Affix 1-inch-wide chrome-plated candle cups (available at antiquelampsupply.com) to the serving ends of a spoon and fork using bonding glue. Let dry for one hour.

Idea 24 Trophy Wine-Stopper: STEP 1 Use a drill to make a $\frac{1}{8}$-inch-wide hole halfway down into a new cork. **STEP 2** Twist off the top of a vintage trophy. Apply Super Glue to the underside of the trophy top's base and the screw that extends from it. **STEP 3** Insert the screw into the cork and twist the pieces together until flush and a tight bond forms. Allow one hour of drying time before using.

Idea 28 TV Tray: STEP 1 Lightly sand and clean a TV tray. Unclip the tray from its legs and stand the legs unfolded atop a drop cloth; lay the tray down atop the drop cloth, too. Spray all sides of the tray and legs with two coats of white primer and two coats of latex paint, allowing at least one hour of drying time after each coat. **STEP 2** Choose a theme for the tray. Gather items that reference the theme, such as a plate and silverware; lay each item on a white surface, then take a high-resolution digital photo of each. Upload, print, and, if necessary, resize the images before cutting them out, trimming as close to the objects' edges as possible. **STEP 3** Using our photo as a guide, experiment with the image placement atop tray. Once you're satisfied with an arrangement, apply Mod Podge to the back of each image with a foam brush before placing the image atop the tray. Smooth out the image with your hand to remove any wrinkles. Repeat for each image and let dry for 15 to 20 minutes. Apply two coats of Mod Podge to the entire tray top (test on a printout first, to make sure the ink doesn't smudge). Allow two hours of drying time after each coat. **STEP 4** Seal the tray and legs with spray varnish. Spray with several light coats, allowing three minutes of drying time after each coat. Allow 24 hours to cure.

Idea 31 Gramophone Pendant Lamp: To assemble this fixture, you'll need a swag lamp kit, three S hooks, each at least two inches long, and a vintage gramophone horn. **STEP 1** Use a scratch awl and a hammer to make three equidistant pilot holes about one inch in from the narrow end of the horn. Drill into those holes. **STEP 2** Assemble the lamp kit following package instructions, and connect the kit's chain to the horn with S hooks before hanging.

Idea 35 Spigot Doorknob: STEP 1 Start by threading the handle onto a 5-by-³⁄₈-inch carriage bolt. **STEP 2** Screw on two nuts, one directly behind the handle to secure it and the other about halfway up the bolt, followed by a washer. If your door doesn't already have a space for the knob, drill a hole about ¹⁄₈ inches smaller than the bolt's diameter. **STEP 3** Screw an inch or so of the bolt into this hole, with the spigot handle facing out; you should have just enough room on the inside of the door to thread another washer and nut onto the end of the bolt. **STEP 4** Tighten the nuts until the washers fit flush against the wood and the spigot handle feels secure.

Idea 44 Book Storage Box: **STEP 1** Each box requires two books—the first will become the outer cover, while the second forms the inner framework. Using an X-Acto knife, carefully remove the entire stack of pages from the first book, cutting as close to the spine as possible. Conceal the now-exposed inner spine with colored paper cut from the first page in the stack, adhering the paper with paper glue. Discard the rest of the stack. **STEP 2** For the inner framework, you'll need to cut four panels from the second book's covers. Use the first book to determine the panels' dimensions. With the first book open flat in front of you, measure the width of the inner spine and subtract ¼ inch. This will be the width of every panel. To determine the length of two panels, measure the length of the inner spine and subtract ½ inch. To determine the length of the other two panels, measure from the outer edge of first book's cover liner to the initial crease of the spine. Cut all four panels from the second book and discard it. **STEP 3** Form a right angle by aligning one long and one short panel, using our photo as a guide. Attach using hot glue, making sure the panels' patterned side faces out. Repeat with the remaining panels. Attach these two right angles to form one rectangle. Cover the framework's top edges with thin strips of colored tape. **STEP 4** Return to the first book and lay it open flat. Stand the framework atop the book's inner back cover and hot-glue in place. Finally, hot-glue the spine to the framework, then let dry.

Idea 52 Three-Chair Bench: STEP 1 Unscrew the seats from the chair backs and armatures of three chairs and set aside. Save the screws. **STEP 2** Line up the chairs side by side, with a few inches between each. Measure the distance from one end of the row to the other, and add four inches to that number. Then measure the depth (from front to back) of one of the seats you just removed. Cut a wood plank with those dimensions (we used a 1-inch-thick, 15-by-58-inch plank here), and sand or miter its edges—or ask someone at your local lumberyard to do it for you. Paint or stain the plank as desired. **STEP 3** Once the plank has dried, place it atop the chairs, center it, and use a pencil to mark where it meets the screw holes in the armatures and the backs of the chairs. (Keep in mind that chairs can age unevenly, so this may require some fiddling.) Remove the plank and drill small pilot holes at each marked point. Put the plank back on top of the chairs, align the pilot holes, and mark where each front chair leg meets the underside of the plank, tracing all the way around the tip of the leg (known as the dowel). Remove the plank. Then, using a drill bit that corresponds to the size of the dowel, bore a 1-inch-deep indentation within your pencil marking, being careful not to drill all the way through the plank. **STEP 4** Apply wood glue to the dowels, position the plank atop the chairs again, and press the bored holes down on the dowels. Screw the back of the plank to the chair backs—and reattach the armatures—with the screws you removed earlier. Place a weight on the plank and let dry overnight.

Idea 65 Hidden Kitchen Cabinet: This project pairs an old metal medicine cabinet with a flea-market painting. **STEP 1** If the cabinet has a mirrored front, carefully remove the glass (be sure to wear gloves, as you may have to break the glass). **STEP 2** Lay your painting facedown on a flat surface, then center your cabinet facedown atop the painting. Use a pencil to mark the cabinet's edges on the back of the frame.

317

STEP 3 With the cabinet still resting on the painting, open it up to expose the back side of the door. Use a permanent marker to mark a dot in each corner of the door, making sure the dots align with the thickest part of the frame. **STEP 4** Lift the cabinet off the painting and lay the cabinet facedown atop a piece of scrap wood. Drill a hole at each of the marked dots, then place the cabinet on top of the painting again, aligning it with the pencil marks on the back of the frame. **STEP 5** Use a drill to drive 1-inch screws through the door holes into the frame. **STEP 6** Mount the unit to the wall using the premade holes in the cabinet's back. If holes don't exist, drill one in each corner.

Idea 94 Kitchen Canister: STEP 1 Go to myfonts.com and download the Home Sweet Home font. Use it to type out the names of pantry staples, adding a decorative flourish if you like, in a word processor, then adjust the type size and alignment to fit your canisters. **STEP 2** Print your documents, following package instructions for 8" W x 11" transparent decal sheets (available at craft stores and on amazon.com). Once the ink has dried, lightly coat each sheet with a thin layer of hair spray, to prevent smearing; let dry. **STEP 3** Cut out and trim each label, then affix to the canisters. Note: The labels won't be entirely waterproof, so when necessary, carefully wash your canisters by hand.

Idea 105 Dresser-Drawer Drink Station: STEP 1 Measure the inside of a dresser drawer to determine its width (from side to side), depth (front to back), and height (base to top). **STEP 2** To create a middle divider, use a jigsaw to cut a piece of wood that measures the depth of the drawer and slightly less than its height. To create a shelf, cut another wood piece that measures slightly less the half the drawer's width and slightly less than its height. Sand the ends. **STEP 3** Using our photo as a guide, insert the shelf and divider into the drawer; screw in place with a drill. **STEP 4** To create a drop-down door, remove any screws holding the dresser's top to its frame; then pop the top off the frame using a rubber mallet. **STEP 5** Cover the drawer unit and door with a coat of primer, followed by two coats of paint, allowing two hours' drying time after each coat. **STEP 6** To install the door, stand the drawer so that its front faces up and its open top faces you. Following package instructions for a piano hinge, attach the door to the back edge of the drawer, as shown above (if needed, trim the hinge with a jigsaw). Make sure the door closes properly before screwing in place. **STEP 7** Install two metal chains, each at least ¼-inch wide, to support the door. Using our photo as a guide, experiment with chain placement before screwing in a set of eye bolts inside the drawer's sides, about three inches from the drawer's front and 1 inch from the top. Use pliers and eye hooks to attach a chain to each eye bolt. Then, on each side of the door, about two inches down from the top edge and 1 inch in from the sides, drill a hole 1 inch wide. **STEP 8** To determine chain length, pull each chain down diagonally to reach the door (the chain needs to hold the door open at exactly 90 degrees). Use pliers to remove excess chain. For each chain, insert the last link into the hole on the door. Drive a screw into the door's side and into the hole, threading the link onto the screw as you go. **STEP 9** To keep the door shut, install safety hooks and eyes on the outside of the door and drawer as shown above. Finish by installing a drawer pull in the center of door's front; then use mounting brackets to hang the station on a wall.

    Idea 126 Photo-Realistic Magnet: For this project, you'll need 12"W x 24" adhesive magnet paper (available on promagproducts.com). **STEP 1** Simply download our PDF (containing the dart and pushpin photos) at countryliving.com/magnets, and print it out on computer paper. **STEP 2** Pull the magnet sheet's paper layer away to reveal the magnet's adhesive side, and place your printed images atop the adhesive. Smooth out any bubbles before cutting out each image with sharp scissors, working close to the images.

    Idea 131 Table Runner: STEP 1 Cut a strip from the drop cloth that measures 14"W x 8' 1" L, iron out any wrinkles, and hem all four edges to create a 13"W x 96"L strip. **STEP 2** Working on one of the strip's long sides and starting at a short end, use a ruler and a pencil to measure and mark one inch at a time; continue until you reach the other end. Repeat on the opposite side of the strip. Next, using your ruler and our photo as a guide, draw a line at each mark, varying the line lengths. At each 16th mark, draw a line that crosses the entire strip. Trace over the lines using a black fabric marker, which dries almost instantly. **STEP 3** Just left of each line that crosses the strip, and working in numerical order, center a six-inch-high number stencil. Affix with stencil adhesive. **STEP 4** Using a foam stencil brush, fill in the stencil with fabric paint and let dry.

    Idea 135 Plastic-Straw Coaster: STEP 1 Using sharp scissors, cut 15 straws of the same color to a length of 5 ½ inches. Repeat with 15 straws in a second color. Next, create a "loom" by drawing 5 ½-inch square on a piece of cardboard. **STEP 2** Beginning with straws of one color, squeeze an end between your thumb and index finger; run the straw between your thumb and finger to flatten. Tape the straw's ends flat along opposite sides of the cardboard square. Continue flattening and taping straws down, side by side, until the square is filled. **STEP 3** Weave the other color straws, one at a time, in and out through the taped-down straws. Push the straws tightly together as you go, to form a checkerboard pattern. **STEP 4** Cut four 7-inch-long strips from a roll of duct tape in a coordinating color. Place 1 strip atop each side of the square so that 1 inch of the tape rests on the straws. Using an X-Acto knife, cut all the way through the tape and the straws on each side to create a clean square that measures approximately 4 inches. Discard the cardboard loom. **STEP 5** Finish off the coaster's edges by cutting four 1-inch-wide strips of duct tape. Fold 1 strip over each edge to create a $\frac{1}{2}$-inch border, trimming as needed, for extra polish.

Idea 143 Sweater Lamp Shade: STEP 1 Cut a large sweater in half along a side seam, removing the sleeves. Pull the resulting rectangle of material tightly around the shade so the fabric meets in the back. **STEP 2** Cut sweater to fit and hot-glue to the shade. **STEP 3** Trim the sweater lengthwise, leaving an inch of overhang at the top and bottom. **STEP 4** Fold the overhang over the shade's edges and secure on the inside with hot glue. For safety, use a low-wattage bulb.

Idea 144 Garden-Party Placemat: STEP 1 Cut each flower off its stem, trimming the back side so it lies flat. **STEP 2** Using our photo as a guide, use chalk to sketch a stem, leaves, or branches. Mark where each flower will go, then set the flowers aside. **STEP 3** Using a needle and green or brown embroidery floss, follow the chalk marks with running stitches. **STEP 4** Attach the flowers with large nylon snaps. At each marked spot, hand-stitch the socket part of a snap onto the placemat. Next, hot-glue the ball part of the snap to the underside of the flower. Let dry for three minutes before snapping the flower onto the placemat. (Note: Simply snap off each flower before dry-cleaning or washing placemats by hand.)

Idea 145 Barnyard Candleholder: STEP 1 Use a drill to make a small pilot hole in the flattest spot on the back of a hollow plastic animal. Align the pilot hole beneath the hole in the bottom of a menorah candle cup. **STEP 2** Secure the cup using a no. 5 screw (its head will rest just atop the cup's hole). Repeat to make multiple holders. **STEP 3** Apply three coats of Krylon's Fusion for Plastic white spray paint, allowing 30 minutes of drying time after each coat. **STEP 4** Place a menorah candle inside each cup.

Idea 150 Spoon Mirror: STEP 1 To begin, you'll need 150 plastic spoons. Place a generous dot of hot glue on the back of the base of the handle of the first spoon. Press the spoon onto the mirror so that its bowl sits just outside the mirror's edge and the handle points toward the center. **STEP 2** Put another dot of hot glue on the back of the second spoon's handle in the same spot, and lay it on the mirror next to the first spoon, so that the widest part of the second one's bowl nestles into the neck of its neighbor. **STEP 3** Repeat steps 1 and 2 all around the mirror's perimeter—just be sure to keep the handles pointed at the mirror's center.

Idea 155 Découpage Lamp Shade: STEP 1 To create a pattern, wrap Kraft paper around your shade and use a pencil to mark its measurements. Lay the paper flat on a table, then follow your marks to draw and cut out the pattern. Place it atop pretty paper (such as wallpaper, gift wrap, or a map); trace the shape in pencil and cut out. Discard the pattern. **STEP 2** Wipe the inside of the shade clean with a dry cloth, then use a sponge applicator to spread a thin layer of Hard Coat Mod Podge onto the area. Carefully apply your paper and smooth to remove bubbles. Let dry for 20 minutes. **STEP 3** Apply a layer of Mod Podge directly onto the paper; let dry for 20 minutes. Apply another layer, then let dry for a full day.

Idea 179 Doily Drink Umbrella: STEP 1 Cut a two-inch-diameter circle out of card stock. Using a glue stick, paste the circle to the solid center of a four-inch doily. **STEP 2** Cut the doily from one edge to the center and bend it into a cone, with the card stock circle on the underside; secure the cut ends with a glue stick. **STEP 3** Hot-glue a wooden skewer to the umbrella's underside, then hot-glue a 1-inch button plug on top.

Idea 180 Picture-Perfect Throw Pillow: STEP 1 Scan and upload the photo to your computer, then place the image in an 8½" x 11" word document. Adjust the image as desired, leaving a half-inch border around it for seam allowance. **STEP 2** Print onto an ink-jet fabric sheet. If necessary, trim the fabric, then cut a same-size piece of backing fabric, like linen or broadcloth. **STEP 3** Pin the two pieces of fabric together, right sides facing. Stitch around the pillow along the seam allowance, leaving a four-inch-wide opening on one side. **STEP 4** Use small scissors to clip the corners, then turn the pillow right side out. Push out the corners, iron out any wrinkles, and stuff the pillow with loose fiberfill stuffing before blind-stitching the opening closed.

Idea 181 Lifesaver Napkin Ring: STEP 1 Simply unscrew the eye screws attached to your curtain rings and lightly sand the painted wood to achieve a distressed finish. **STEP 2** Use a red or blue Sharpie marker to draw four equally spaced stripes around each ring. Let dry for five minutes. **STEP 3** With a set of alphabet stamps and a black ink pad, stamp the phrase of your choice onto each ring. **STEP 4** Wait another five minutes, then coat the rings with a clear acrylic spray. Let dry for 20 minutes before sliding onto napkins.

Idea 193 Drink-Umbrella Pendant Lamp: Begin by cutting off the bottom half of an umbrella stick and discarding. **STEP 1** Spray a 4-inch-wide area in the middle of the lantern with acid-free adhesive; then use the remaining end of the stick to poke a hole in the paper, pushing the open umbrella down against the lantern until it fans out flat. Hold in place until a bond forms. **STEP 2** Reaching inside the shade, apply a drop of tacky glue to the end of the umbrella stick and slide on a small plastic tri-bead to secure. **STEP 3** Trim off any excess stick and discard. Continue adding all the umbrellas in the same manner, overlapping them as you go. **STEP 4** Wait three hours for the acid-free adhesive to dry; then spray the outside of the globe with a coat of paper-friendly clear lacquer. Allow one hour to dry.

Idea 267 Painted Hand Mirror: STEP 1 To fashion this piece, go to countryliving.com/mirror and print our template, sized to fit an 11¾″ W x 16″ H mirror. Trim the template as directed and place the resulting hand-mirror shape atop contact paper. **STEP 2** Outline, then cut out. Peel away the backing and center the shape, sticky side down, on the mirror. **STEP 3** Spray the mirror's surface with a coat of no-prime acrylic paint—we used Montana Gold's Bazooka Joe. Let dry for 30 minutes; then peel off contact paper.

Photography Credits

Melanie Acevedo: 130 top right, 163, 310

Lucas Allen: xii top left and bottom right, 17, 18, 29, 70 top left and bottom left, 74, 76, 81, 86, 87, 89, 99, 102, 105, 128, 133, 151, 157, 166, 173, 187, 220, 226-227, 238, 252-253, 256 top left, 265, 267, 274, 275, 278 right, 283, 284, 306

Sang An: 180, 186

Burcu Avsar: 70 bottom right, 104, 110, 118, 130 top left, 148, 159, 161, 260

Quentin Bacon: 69

Christopher Baker: 91, 170, 251

Roland Bello: 40, 90, 209, 303

Amber S. Clark: 3, 21, 36, 41, 60 (both photos), 143

Colin Cooke: 160

Roger Davies: xi top right, 171, 203, 204-205, 234, 259, 282, 290, 307, 309

Tara Donne: 256 bottom left, 292

Miki Duisterhof: ii, 30, 32, 58, 59, 63, 64, 107, 113, 141, 152, 154, 168, 177, 198, 240 bottom left, 250, 261, 300

Lisa Romerein: 6, 46-47, 201

Victor Schrager: 33

Kate Sears: 52, 53 (both photos)

Anson Smart: 211

Seth Smoot: 158, 164, 174, 197

Tim Street-Porter: 116, 119, 155, 165, 270, 285, 287

Robin Stubbert: 45

Studio D: Ben Goldstein: xi top left, 162; Karl Juengel: 15; Lara Robby: 28, 115, 130 bottom right, 181, 185, 189, 212, 213, 281; Alison Gootee: 51, 273; Philip Friedman: 112

Jonny Valiant: 4, 126

Mikkel Vang: 49, 65, 191, 192, 193, 206-207, 222

William Waldron: xi bottom right, 42, 153, 136, 200, 228, 229, 286, 311

Björn Wallander: 8, 10-11, 26-27, 38, 50, 75, 85, 94-95, 100, 101, 103, 106, 121, 134, 138-139, 146-147, 194, 230, 235, 237, 258, 266, 272, 276, 280, 294, 295, 298, 301, 308

Richard Warren: 240 top left, 240 bottom right, 247, 254

Wendell T. Webber: 68, 98, 216

Polly Wreford: 37

Andrea Wyner: 73, 111

Front Cover: (clockwise from top left): Burcu Avsar, Björn Wallander, Kate Mathis, Lucas Allen, Björn Wallander, Laura Moss, Susan McWhinney, Victor Schrager, Roger Davies, Ben Goldstein/Studio D, Kana Okada, Kate Mathis, Laura Moss, Tim Street-Porter, Kate Sears, Wendell T. Webber, Miki Duisterhof, Lucas Allen, Max Kim-Bee, Sang An

Front Inside Flap: Miki Duisterhof

Back Cover: Kate Mathis (top), Amber S. Clark (bottom left), Max Kim-Bee (bottom right)

Index